MIND FOR THE BARRICADES ARCADE

George E Harris

Published by William Cornelius Harris Publishing
In collaboration

with

London Poetry Books

Supporting Mental Health in Performing Arts

ISBN 978-1-911232-64-3

William Young
34 Birchwood Close, Bordesley Road SM4 5NH

London Poetry Books

This publication is dedicated to, and is very much for the love I have and had with Alison O'Melia who sadly passed in December 2020.

To Our Families Harris and O'Melia
To my Dad John Harris who sadly passed in 2024

To all the collaborations Alison and I did.
To Walt and David who brought us together
We worked on so much through our lives together especially with
Rookery Ensemble, which continues as a working music and words project.
To all those on board the Rook Family Ship - Erik, Mark, Mitzy, Victoria, David, Hilary, Jess, Demi, Annabella, K,Walt, Lorin, Agata, keith and Alan plus, others like Jono and Paul who supported with the sound.

To all the folk who supported us Me and Alison in so many ways and those who supported me also, too many names to mention here,
but you know who you are...

To all the poets, artists, singers, musicians,
Vagabonds, promoters and puppeteers I know.
To Tracey Meek RIP
Pat Flowers for help
To Keith Bray and Jason Why for being who you are.

CONTENTS

Interspersed with Photographs and Art also by

George E Harris - links images and sounds
www.worldofsurprises.co.uk

And bouncing back
The edit of bumping into something
Spin spin spin
The merry go round
I cry and see
Circles of intrigue
Cycles of season

IN MEMORY OF THE MASTS

In a blink of an eye
I look all around
You had such a full one
Sometimes on the edge of rebellion.

Not always the intention
As you always spoke up
Spoke your mind
It was fully yours and only.
OOOOOOOOOOOOOOO

Riding high in the moment
Bouncing off the singing bowls
Into the shimmering waves of water
Wild rivers somewhere up north or far out…

Spinning along in deep rooted social consciousness
Skill of performing out
The cabaret through hoops
Moustache on displaying on non-gender specific...

In memories of the masts
Walking along in the morning
The airs flowing through
Rattling the loose barriers up the slope.

Spirit hanging on now with warmth
Not sure how, but is, I'm keeping this up.
My pretence in working through it all
Close my eyes and now taken back
To the car park on the coastal flank.

Your harmonica soars through
The passage of gusts in the masts
The dreams are ours to keep
Coming back into this moment
We're in the era of backdrops
And fore fronted expressions in rebellious passion
Let's take our stand at this time…

NO CITIES AWAITING

Lost today amongst the bare shelves
Haunted in fact and factor
Talking over the never ever
Inside this hole that's being circumnavigated
Of those looking in we're anything but
The ones you think we are …

In halves halls nothing else venting spirals deep
Heart beat feeling we're awaiting
The physical loose galore…

Oh oh oh it's not the freaking time
No cities awaiting
Turning up the maximum
Come back into the light then they say it's too bright
Listen to the wall of noise
Every sense is tingling over itself in curious finds.

Dead sofas on walkways
Upturned kitchen cabinets aching asking
For a time, we have
Every appliance is discarded by the roadside
Demonstration to change the bill
We're not out yet this is turning
So, against the society built.

No cities floating above postcards coming
But left to be found many years later
Concealed cities in exercise
Faded signs staring at the floor
Staring at something else not looking at each other
Waiting for this delayed train
Just bumped into someone you know
Let's get the bus and up the escalator
Around to the stop it's so busy …

You just manage it within 10 minutes
On a scale of futile city
The hole it's in …
Empty sequence of the bounce.

The couple walk up the slope at the circus
Many years more now gone by
Two shopping bags and pull along trolley
A suitcase on wheels.
The slow motion gives us time to think
Observe the impatience of some others
Forever brief I will remember this course in kindness
And Miss my sweetheart in the mists…

ISLETS OF LANGERHANS

In wonder of the exotic locations
Well it's a destination grouping
In peace now a beautiful power
Surges forth in those love of humanity.

Traveller taking stock of spirits
Surrounding holding close within
Our hearts, but high walking closes with an equal.
In the three dimensions sprung a cluster
Of cells in their thousands
Sing for the Islets of Langerhans
Celebrated rhythm closing and loss of beta cells…
Sing for the Islets of Langerhans

In the peninsula growth of landscape maintained
On the spherical edge forming
The Islet and blood flows.
Trouble is now the outside comes in equal pressures
Charged, but we maintain the
Relationships of structures and understandings.

So many contradictions come
But it's the basis of our love and movement
Wishes of the immortal
And those that now live in-between
We tangle the many valleys and hills of our locations…

Trails we follow of the true artist
Believing in the connections we make
Time will tell in the tales and remembrance
Of A. Raven So Dear…

Sing for the Islets of Langerhans
We walk ever closer to the destinations near and far
Sing for the Islets of Langerhans
We talk and sit holding what it is we Love and Fear
Sing Out for the Islets of Langerhans
We dance and shout out for the spirit so revenant
Now we all Sing for the Islets of Langerhans …

FOUR SEALS

Guardians of the light
Ebb and flow of the bay
Golden light on the edge
We two are reading words on the slope.

Observers of our task
Dawn trace ash with Seeds to grow
A, my love you are flying to the land
Of sea and green hills.

Brittle time of beauty move
Silence except the tide and breeze
Laid to rest / so breathe…

Scatter and sow
Movement of thoughts
Golden green of grass slopes
Blue turquoise of the ocean sounding.

Birds singing rabbits on the land
Ebb and flow out in the bay
Your spirit is with us in every conversation
Move and flow every thought goes.

And transfixes the moments
Ghosts and living it
Out to dance the morning light.

SLOWLY AND DOWN

By chance in the click
Up the brow and over the view
Hot day in clear blue
With a single cloud just resting
On the wires communicating
Through the golden lands

Sense of the drama out there
And inside of the paper blinds
Recycled standards fittings
Inside and advanced over the tracks

Staring out of this carriage
Waiting on the slowly and down
Slowly and down

Upturned lime bike now back
Scratching heads and morning coffee
The rock n roll gangster walks
Out from this carriage
Down the road on hand
To make some moves

The city scene
splays out
Slowly and down…

Swimming in the broken texts
Hair flows like straw
By the hands held up
With attentions from the megaphone preacher
There out again offering that blessing of the missing

To make some sense did I just see that?
Came out of the guy's hand
And just flew down the track …
My mind's on the Cornish choir
In calling keeping it slowly and down

It's by chance on the click
Let's talk about the things
Holding the revolution up
Into its new compartment
Situation slip handed out in the waiting room
Let's come and see it work through the new horizon

Thinking about home
Thinking a place
Thinking on a concept
Thinking about the real
Thinking about the false avenues
Thinking about what we have
Taking it moving it
Slowly and down
Talking with people
I haven't done so for many years.

Thinking about place
Thinking about where I am
Thinking around the possible
Thinking about nothing in particular
Thinking in the direct meaning
Thinking around it all

In direct feeling and emotional bonds
Within the deep click and glitch
Slowly and down
Circles on the hill down to the sea
I'm entering another tale
Moments of national crisis and frozen jubilations
Going to take it slowly and down
Forever in the conversation

Oh, A Raven we will be in the forever time crossing
Borders and brows, smile and hold in mind
The choir of the sky
Singing out in cut away slithers
Packaged in a fancy cloth
Holding treasure in small cases of tone recall…

Dipping into madness and sleep holds
Dreaming of hills and sound dust
The figure walks towards me
Blurred when close to see repeated heralds
Bones of self-expressions
Slowly and down.

MY PHYSICAL STAR

Under this rich blanket
I stare up into its depth
Flashing light
Off to the left
And dog howls to the right

In the minutes outside
Most of it silent
Tears spread down
In the thoughts flying through the sky

The shadows of trees
Spread under moonlight
Selfie nearby with visitations
Feeling through the landscape

Physical star
Looping in and out
Tears run down my cheeks
Next day too much cover to see
I stare out at the webs in bushes

Imagined spires in the trees
Nightscape beginning to move
My love walks within
Moon crescent streams.

Light breeze of leaves
around the face
Circle the stone crown upon the seats
The angels are flitting in and out
But you're sitting nearby listening
To this piano work and rain outside
Sparking reverence in feelings of silence…

I need the sound and just sit and listen
You're there now up with all who were with you
The drift and scratched feeling
Oh, so low sometimes…

But I know
In listening…
Put it to pen and paper…

I need the sound and listen to move
This twitch inside has a roar
That I need to protect
It goes on and we move through tone
But the love never goes and I see
Wish I could have written that when you
Was still the physical star…

UNSTEADY READY

Love notes thrown as a paper plane
Landed in the bush nearby
Flapping out in the breeze.
I Wanna Be Yours.

Just off into the city,
Snake man's nearby.
Sounds of the silver blade slide
In a whoosh of air crossing the street.

Smiles on and never changed
As we move on up.
In my mind it gives me a shiver,
Keeping an eye reminds me of you
In a spirit message to the world.

Here now listening to the primitive painters
Just feeling elated on the bench.
Staring into spaces of deep consideration
At all times over the sequence.

Eyes ripped up,
But only in the mirror walk.
Steeped in overthinking,
I need to stop until the machine wakes.
Instantly it's then strenuous and impacting the flow.

Signs indicating heads to be taken away,
Upturned eyes staring out in a fish like manner.
Sampled horror branches squeezing
And spirited into the ether.

Danger plateaus just out of reach,
Served up image looking on in dispirited joy.
Banging the beat out on track,
Observing outside in calm with a butterfly light.

And as the bite beams back,
What on earth was I thinking?
Some distance in the contemplation,
I wish you were here right now,
So so so with the unsteady ready.

ACCORDION SPIRIT

The fox came visiting late this afternoon,
Sniffing and resting around the pots
In the garden out back…
I looked out whilst doing the dishes,
Amount of peace in this scene.

Been reading all day the moon now
Peeking over and through the trees opposite
Its cross over time of gold and it's got darker in time.

I cooked my evening meal
Could hear barking outside
Hope the fox is ok
Accordion spirit making time to visit
And go again just to see in a moment.

I'm flat out today
A wave of tiredness has come over me
I need the dance to come back and will one day
For now, this is the way in small crests over the crust.
Oh, you Accordion Spirit please come back
And make the dance again.

In the time now
That we couldn't imagine
But knew things were moving.
Chitter chatter outside possibilities and in roads.

I’ve been numbing myself again took two days away
Clearing my head and we come back to that again.
I need you Accordion Spirit
To bring back the tango
Back into the gateway we danced
Clearer minds and just move sowing the round.

SPEED QUEEN INTERPRETATIONS

Today remembering the conversations, we had,
The stories you told, driving exploits
All those years gone in your pocket rocket
Speed Queen conversations of gaining signals
And then you're off beating the men
At their own game down the high way spine.

So many sides to your life
From doing the books for the outlaws
To those contemporary music improvisations for all.
A life I was not part of until your last 10 …
With spirit we move and recall the flight…

A simultaneous life you lead
Of driving across the mid European mountains
On a trip to help the Romanian Children
Blowing your clarinet to a cow whilst dancing
And partying in a field somewhere some place
To the heights of marching for people's rights…

Takes me now to the concept of
Salsa metal and dancing carnival cows
In the green fields of festival time
Fleet artists to music hearts
Beating the revolutionary banner
Your passion in speed queen conversations
Was equal in every measure …

You always said your family line
Led back to the west coast Pirate Queen
You loved to think so
And good energy to keep that going.
Your determinations in these last months
Are proofs of your fierce, strength of will…

Traits to imagine come down the line.
Sounds and rhythms, poetry and speech
Mind and power in creation
Always figured and maintained.
A soul of beauty of the earth,
Sky, water and fire to the mind.
Forever embodied in a long and ancient path.

Even in times of illness
Your will to drive out injustice was still in sight
But at times had taken a back seat rest
We had to keep some stories for us and no one else.
My love for you the pirate queen of the stars
And so installed the mystic and ventures in belief…

THE CONVERSATION

The Conversation we had
The conversation we have
The conversation that's been recorded
The dialogue that's from memory
The dialogue that's been written
The conversation that's been observed
In the obscured parallel
The conversation that's cut up
Re ordered and transfigured
Obsessed over transfixed
Lips synched or vocal coached
Is it murder or is it love
The conversation we have with the spirits
Flying or rested
The one with one's self
A conversation in spirals
To our best friends or the person passing
Maybe simultaneously hoping that
Conversation will spark another
Or is it silence…

We can't end it there
It's an on-going conversation
Of over lapping words many in fact
Each word speaks to the one after
In a round of so much...

The conversation through listening
A conversation through a calendar
Dated to revolutionary moments in history
The conversation with a photograph of you
One of many but especially the one taken in the park
The conversation you have with an alter ego
The conversation we have with harmony
The conversation we have with disharmony
The conversation we have with spirits please hold on_
The conversation we have with loves
Do ictus silent now (no)
The conversation we have on the roundabout
The conversation we have on a bus
This conversation on the obsessive bench
The conversation we continue with the spirits
Hoping they never go away
The conversation we have on a train
The conversation that doesn't ever happen really
The conversation in my head
The intensity of such never aligns
Let's get the graph paper out
And map it more precisely
The conversation we have
With a past and future aligned
Can never tell when that may happen
The conversation I had today
It's in the performance
Deep down to the word
Spread to border plains over horizons

The conversation you overhear
But now forgotten but steady it may come back…
Partial glimpse into an individual's narrative of that day
The conversation we put on hold
The conversation we had
The conversation with memory
The conversation that's happy and now sad
The conversation that's angry and then not so bad
The conversation through fear
The conversation through need
The conversation that's full of passions
The conversation on a long history
The conversations on the recent past
The conversations now so still
The conversation to a future self
To Continue in The Conversation…

PICTURED SLIPPED

We might fall a little
For a while, but the roll
Did stand up at the end.

Fallen trees out right
Taken on the plains, corners, parks
And in the forests surrounded
They're family and speaking
Through channels of debris
Fungus under growth
Hoping it's not the worst.

Communications in myths and legends
Abound and sayings of symbolic
Nature in the falling
The spirals inside interpret
The ancient and your touch of hands
On in the lay of the lines…

We sing of the pictured slipped
Oh, so vital our eyes observe
We sing of the pictured slipped
Today its somewhere over the way.

We might fall a little
For a while, but the roll
Did stand up at the end…

We might fall a little
It's been in the eternity spring
Playing out the songs
On the side sprawls
But speaking to the air…

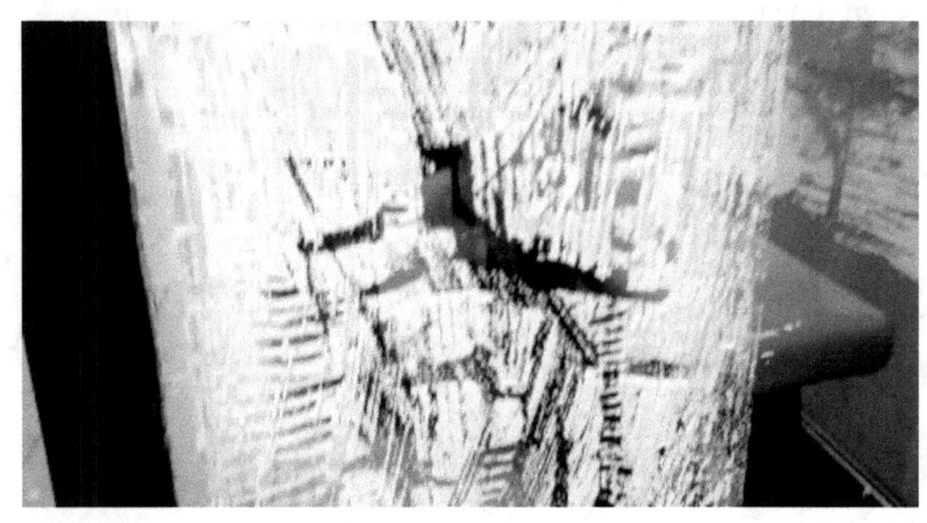

GIANT BUTTERFLIES IN THE SNOW

Temporary beauty in the days going by
Passing drift shifting sheets
Blankets over the land in a while…

The giants are out today
Fluttering over the lands out back.
Voices are coming out of the skies
Singing high on sheer faces.

The moment caught in full colour
Sequence and mind's eye tranquil
View out back
Giant butterflies in the snow
Cross over zone living twilight…

Spirits of flight, spirits of the earth,
Hands on the sounds created
Zone of glass fragility chambers
A surface treating into the deep time.
The spirit voices come and sing
Speak of many and few things.
Amongst our rooms perched on these hills
Those contemporary movements
In the temporary slides.
The pluck and awe
Conjure our moments in the mourning.

Views out back in the snows
Over our heads deep in thought
Sound takes us away somewhere
And above we discover in groove.
Views out back giant butterflies in the snow
A sequence of moments clashing forward

We hold it high in mind
Out of the blue constellations
Come forth in skyward wonders
On high wires rhythms in mind
In cosmic loads and the open roads.

Compiled thoughts in a moment
Float out on to this page
Writing has kept going in this
Process of out and in those flights over the land.

Short lived and hanging in there
But burning bright on the time
Exposed over the land.
Fluttering shapes against the temporal

Land, fields and gardens
up high and down so low.
Its o
All part of the process and possess, paralysis
Do we now feel fine?

And look to those better futures
Through uncertainties empty and fright
We take the moment to…

Flutter up and about to create
The cycle is in motion
We take our flow and sing the round
Those words out back
And in every ounce of our moment…

CRASHING IN DISTRACTED SIGNALS

Distant signals coming through
Strange sounds from a far-off land
That feels so close to home
Channel hopping into white noise

And back and forth over the buzzer
Wailing voices heard
On this journey down the valley
Turned violin into industrial drum

The buzzer hits again
The intensity of the person in front
Strange voices speaking over machine gun rattle
I look out its bright and sunny down the hill

The conflicted sounds seem so far away
But all could be involved
Dark times are back again
Through water ground over broken lands

Laughter comes now in strange tone
Hesitant and pauses
Over repeated folk sound hyper fast rhythms
Then more machine gun sounds ring out
But there's nothing
But sunshine today.

Sounds coming down through this bus
From a mobile device out front
Sparking my thoughts of crashing conflict
In distracted signals over the lands.

Yes, it's more coming
We don't need another
But it's happening now over the lands
I'm now thinking of those stuck in the middle
The ones who have not any control.

THE ROOK STARES ON ANOTHER DAY

The heartbreak keeps coming
Alongside those memories and great times over.
The Rook sits on the statue's head and stares on…
These days now in-between
Now reaching through the week
Before we lay thee down…

Listening to the composers that inspired
Listening to the people
Those were talked about and listening
To the new that were passed on to savour…

Cutting some ropes to raise the bridge
Every so often I sit there crying
Triggered in the small moment
I sometimes wonder when it's getting clearer.

The cycle rounds will come through
The industrial interpretations,
Rooks stare and blues triangles.
The bulbs are now blooming except the one
Let's keep it there and see what grows…

Low flying in the night
Its 2am wow that was loud
Too much for some, but it's taking me
To those next lines, then over and down.

Folksongs bloom on sofa lines
Has been my point of rest.
Over the months even years now
Since you fell on and off, back and forth…
Barking silence outside
With my orange light on minor warmth
In the hints of listening
Rain and wind tensions spin songs…

The low flying continues into more movement …
The heartbreaks do keep coming
No question where it steers
Just holding one on the verges…
I today a week sometime on
Breathe in a walk out of many
As a rook stares on through the other days…

DEAD EYES

It’s a Super Moon Conspiracy move on move on.
All hail the deep driver in the slow plunge.
They come every minute,
Like all the 10% sale shifts that mesmerize my brain.

Is it a sonic extinction
Through the rain-drenched street?
Garbled goods made through company’s materials.
Every week it goes home through on coat supply.
It’s the greatest ever all-inclusive invention.

Insufficient housing block,
Workplace social club flattened.
Mr. Hexagon Face is on the phone again,
Trouble is being brewed to order.

Now, now, now we’re on a right one today.
Thought waves have just missed
The best line ever made.
The local’s gone old man passing just staring in.
Learn how to infest the coming electric vehicle.

Trails in schemes not yet reached.
Trauma in far-fetched seats,
Secrets to exchange
With Dead Eyes to exploit.

Clown shoes upshot
A mystery surveillance operation.
Aimless then so direct in the exclusions monitoring.
Plastic stars in the gutter,
Tiny gardens on porch covers.
Juggler on the crossing, flatbed trucks waiting.

Tears of the homeless, I see people just walking.
Today we count and write on repeat.
Yeah, you're now gone it's a feeling going.
Genius moves in the not so half belligerents.

TOP FIELD

I said I said top field was were
The Mode used to
Come and cause havoc...

Making each exploit the bizarre story it is
But what I should have said
Were the gems that made this
So magic is you...

Deep in our folk tale
Exploring the edges of green
A world of surprise
Masts on being so free...

Adding so much
As listening through time
Boxes on calendar mind
With sparks of word and sound
To now still here with you...

THE OPERATIVE

As entering a normal job,
Mark the network just maintaining cover,
Misleading those whom have become friends.

Inside crimes committed,
Moving morning in blind circles.
Shouting out the silence in loud taking of the tunnel.

Gains in omnipathic nature to be
The operative holding selfish horizon.
In a pack missing
Discovered after years of purges.

Follow do you have it do you want some help.
The chorus rings up pressures of a well-trodden path.
Is it so called manly
To follow a team in packs?

Your shifting focus throwing anger shapes,
Diverting some attentions in sympathetic un gestures.
Hounds will howl – it's not on my watch.

Recruitments of gangster managers,
Shock assistants
And fork lift assassins for the mob.
All years of misleading those you love, just living it up.

Lifestyle highlights and operating a trade in gifts.
Send it down to Dalston Market, open the junction.
Weapons shoot through to a thing that gets twisted.

Pinned down qualified do you know?
On the bridge replaced as the project goes on.
When the next operator just comes stepping up.

RISE IN THE HARMONIUM DRONE

Sometimes it feels a need to hide.
Tuck away into a place no one knows.
Shapes show that we go through every day,
Stealing the ounce of time to move on.

It seems the illness is getting worse.
Each day the triumphs of holding your hand
With speaking times and keeping afloat.

I wish to make the fact clear we are here
With battles won and a love that will always be.

In and out, back and forth, searching the cure.
Your rise in harmonium drone,
Music and sound on the dragon step ladders of yore.

On the slopes from the hole,
In times to stand up on the interlude.
Foretold in pencil drawings of spectacular lining.

Sometimes it feels each day
Feeds against heart bent strings
In the lasting persecutions.

The want to come forth in harmonium drone,
Taking the harmony and rise,
Upon streams out of this circus town.

SOMETHING HAPPENED

The day that fell into a continuous argument,
On and off building each hour,
Fraying on edge.
The repeated motions seemed to echo
The on-going crisis outside.

The bigger picture rode on to speak,
Just occurring in movement frequency
And treatments all so often,
Overlapping the circles building.
As it gave way in roving raps,
It’s gone beyond any comic turn
That could break the illusion.

The processing of information
In incredible stirs.
It occurred to me
From decreasing ripples into waves.
High in the tit for tat,
Just repeating it over near crushing.

The record clicks, jumps glitches,
Missing some sound information.
Giving up on the jets,
Yes, now and never on those alternative scopes.
Oh, forever burning some trouble on these hooks.

Will the horses ever run again?
Now watching in the corner café.
Fancy dressed kings and kings with queens,
Edges of the gold dissolved into plastic cups.

Hang them up at given time slots,
Feeding click bait,
Ignoring some reasoning.
Those faces turn red as the anger pursues
Some form as it starts
To feel patronised and cornered.

Assuming airs in the calm breeze,
On a day like that you need to get away.
Run with kites
Up on the hills feeding the soul,
Needing to dry the points,
But not rise to the off the cuff tattle.

Time puts things down into the perspective,
Holding measures that correctly
Show stretches on a late shift.

Horizons glow as it all gives sway,
Falling to brazen talk…
The shuttered poke,
Climate trolls, Forever germinating,
The land beyond this.

Hidden in the corner
With the gargoyles on the terrace.
We cover the markings of hearing
Them sing in tones of deep frustration.
Discussions carry through now to a touch
Of depending and over toning!

Will the horses ever run again?
Now watching in the corner café.
Fancy dressed kings and kings with queens,
Edges of the gold dissolved into plastic cups.

THE PROJECTIONIST

The light flashes, flickers into the cavernous pit.
Out picks the reels
Spliced and time watched
Through periscope eyes.
Beating pulse to change the next reel
On the over reached day.

Seats in cigarette fogged rows, ghost sittings
To view the greatest showing.
The film today is taken of the journey
To daily clocking in.
A New Wave Classic of unknown proportions.

No but there’s not a sign of the Black and White
Heroes and heroines,
But Super Animations
In a sub divided honeycomb of screens.
Backlit with polished advertising relived,
Brandishing that next plastic outfitting.

Projected new reality,
An implosion in the bright horizons.
A song and dance to sell the fantasy
With horror trailers hitched on.
Cold valley to the screen doors,
Bills shouting get the next fix.

Friendly unconvinced smile of a fast enterprise.
A past cinematic reality strikes a chord with us.
On blending with the new this seems
Now so distant from the consciousness.

Up the stepladder on to the next levels,
The projectionist clings
To the ghost sparks and rattle of film roll.
'There was once a team that did this a few of us now,
It's just me and the one down below.'

Operating the machinery imagining the roles they are playing.
Shift pattern to run the length of a day,
But changing the digitised voice ever so often.
The structure of a whole experience mustered,
Electric adventures in this dark wonder.

Listening out hearing the crowds roar,
The shock of a tense scene,
But there is silence in this now fully automated room.
Up behind the seating
Watching over and into the eyes of all.

A silence that is stirred momentarily
In burrs and springs around.
Taking the present definitions
And sci-fi holds into ways of future viewing.
Grasping the cinema that can be experienced
In a full degree without ever waking.

Feeding the fix in our dreams
Through contracts drawn when born.
Each experience we now draw
Comes from the fantasy being fed in.

The projectionist now sits at home being fed streams,
Which in turn get diverted out.

We've become the film and we live the day,
We've become the film and we live the day,
We've become the film and we live the day.

A chant of the mastered out in the fields,
A chant in the virtual a reality to all,
A chant in the freedom lost in this not so fantastic dawn.

HYPER REALITY STAR

In the on-going melee of this existence
We trail the thoughts of what could be
Into what is or what ever in the time being

Lying here in the circle of remembering
Trying to see ways to a future
Listening to a revolutionary record
It's 33rpm and it's a way out with a passion…

Covering so many bases
But the scream is always there under my skin.
Many previous submissions but it has to be
Slightly off kilter to penetrate this crust…

Surface raps suppressing the day
Time is not to bury the head
So much is out there
Breaking the walls and charging forward
For the memory is still there.

We need to take the juggler and reader
Up to the plateau near the casting zone …
Up high to the skies in a visionary depth
Our hyper reality stars
Rise each melody and chord
Movements and insights reprised …

The hyper reality is in a condition hearing…
But the stars keep shining
Trying to gain some sort of normality
In whatever that means…

Our Hyper Reality Stars live in the
Mind-set of the in-between…
No terms and conditions just insights into
Our day-to-day clashing and moments to uphold…

Yes, we are told
There are no conditions
That can't be solved
No messages except the ones
Put on mute…

We are in need of
Songs for the raven
Downtown…
You Gone!

All the planes are suspended in mid-air...

IN GRID REFERENCE

Today the sky changed and
A cat appeared in the line of sight
Up within the clouds on high above this city

My father passed in his sleep
That same afternoon
Some distance deep down
So many people here and around
I felt deep cold in the pit of being
Now out in the warmth of bustling hoards

Missed calls and then
I'm now speaking with my brother
Having come out of work
Voices crossing over
Whispering shadows coming round

Deep into the body mists
Walking choirs whistling
In echo going underground

Be careful out there
Thin mind springs are propped
Waiting to slip and fly off
So, slow
The jelly legs in the sun.

Now dads grid reference
Has moved from higher croft
To barn lower in the region of river turns

Tales of whistling in the garden
Nightingales are predominant guessing well
Spirits fields and tales of fooling others
Made us smile so

The wind is carrying sound over the brow
Distant and close baring's of time
Deep sounds late at night
In the countryside
Low rumble coming down the chimney
And the sound goes by into the distance.

Watching the folk songs
Play out tonight and others to follow

Tales of a long-lost black cockerel
Blackrock banished for scaring
The younger siblings
Growing up on the farm holding
But would come back as
A ghostly tale in appearance over

In truth memories
Through the fog banks
Over the land and sea.

I see you by the tree
Upon the cliff, over the sea
And I speak to you…

Now the moon is full
In clear night
Flare over croft and peaceful skies.

A memory just shot out
Of dad taking us to a gig
Down by the coast
One of our first of many
Reggae beats in the winter gardens
In those days when folk could still smoke
Inside a sweet smell of something
Not known for a time
The big beat and bass booms
Early 80s late 70s and so…

Now in the present I'm listening
To mum speak and read
In the kitchen morning of the day
Reading loud her book of the moment
Each day we lose something
But grasping the thoughts of now
Then the rooks are on the line
In respect as we drive by
Silent going by I stare out.

SILVER SHARP MORNING

Chaos plays and breathes
Into this valley, deep constructs
Held in estimated calculations.

Light clears into the yard
Blinding glare over the brow
And I feel warmed from the cool cool air
Its harpsichord place tingled on reach.

Truth on what am I doing
Where am I going?
Into the silver sharp morning
Out stitched remember thinking on this road
How glad I was to be with you A Raven

Out in the time of witness
Following our hearts in the bloom
It's pouring today
Like it has over many times
Down on the bank into the depth.

Storm of words across the lifting
Unknown character rushes by
Passed to the second on
Stammer over on those words
Tripping the fantastic
Now spreads the light…

MIND SPIKE'S

ANOTHER DAY IN MIND SPIKES

Started with a painted circle
Marking a hole in the ground
Traveller's contracts supplied
Overlapped text repair specialist
Repeated knots and Lurline stretch…
Get on with it
I hear just behind me…

Today another day in mind spikes
Along the line of many more
I'm feeling, waves of sickness in the pit
Functioning depression attributes
Held and coming in waves
But I'm walking watching
People float by all held on by threads.

Heading somewhere or just nowhere
But I am glad I can physically write this moment down.
Wanting it sung in the round or just lie it down
In the line of the rest
But I want it all to dance.

And just be
Never to have changed
And thy still with
And just be, and just be
And just be, and just be, it gets me too!

WISH I STILL HAD SOME MUNDANE TIME

To kiss those lips once again
In the eternity spring
My love is in the weather outside
Free in the wind and nature's yearnings.

Thinking out by the back door of the old house
I said I love you and meant it forever
Now listening to the wind
In the windows as we travel
Now committed in this journey.

Simultaneously someone in the seat opposite
Is writing and looking over
Is their concept of wonder?
I see out the side of my eye.

I'm off and now it's just memory
And someone's dancing at the stop
Life in sacred pulse
I feel the glow now.

Yesterday I rediscovered a photograph
It was of you and the ensemble of time
In full dialogue
Oh, my love
Finding us
I just wish for some mundane time with you again.

DOCUMENT ON THE ASTRAL PLAIN

This Sunday morning could be any morning I say
'We've all been doing that lately'
After obsessional talking was expressed by
The lady at the bus stop this morning.

Waiting on her Express for mother
From corner shop on end of street
My bus comes and I wish her well in the quest
Thinking I would not buy such a paper
Stepping on the bus.

But what an attitude to have
It's just snobbery
It's just part of the framework
Of their life like many others
Its what's always gone on?

Further on like the dancing lady
Up the parade
The obsessional man on a laptop
In front seat work ethic note taking
Me just writing this and looking…
Documenters on the astral plain…

Lady walking her mop of a dog
In the dark corners of the luxury gap
It was constant corner to corner.

Couple get out of cab right early
Morning arrival from airport
Scanning the technology to find some way
Looking as though they should be clubbing.

The drums are beating
Into the land
Ley the heart as the stream widens
Into the mouth
Those singing out in the dark
Storm is raging around.

In time shifting round us all
Meeting the guardians
Of the fantastic out at one.
Combined surprise
Figures in circles reading aloud
In the opposite window…

In the post storm ridden land tensions high and free
Heads lay on the side staring down
In the valley spray branches remain spread
Searching out into knowledge…

MIND FOR THE BARRICADES ARCADE

Gratitude triumphs in that furnace place,
Neat trimmings simply put in
The re-arranged and re-read maps.
Forgone conclusions and traces
On partial surface duplicated,
Clumping at the horses,
Let's meet at the Iron Duke
Just on the cusp
In comic timings and faced up ways.

Now with the Pomelo on the Wyatt Park Road dream,
Way off south out of reach the trees are waiting,
Hoarding on street corners
In discarded celebration until next time.
Lone birds staring then rising,
Unheard treatments of news perceptions.
Comet transport waves where
The universe is now being played out.

Pimlico disorder in passports checkpoint
Chasing with something that was lost in years on trials.
Running the length on absolute
Sceptical and damning research.
Principalities of pound shop gangsters
Behind the doors all in blue,
Down the length of antique whitewashed streets.

Broken furniture on side verges,
Chucked out and memories etched into the fabric.
Burning witness buried in the misled years
And surfaced when needed.
Lightning strikes when its time,
Comment is now required to increase the traffic flow.

Yes
On the bridges reviewed in every crossing
With the small-faced pastings.

The chips are down on sanctuary place,
Thrown over the shoulder
On viewing the magpie eye.
Ways of making up stories through
Breathing a week's notice.
Escalator tangos, as the assistant looks blank
On these mechanical runs.

Disorder in a Victoria departure slapped
On the face of that tube traveller.
What after you barged into
The same food carrying ground worker.

Carriers smashed to the floor and shouts of out of order.
So many concerned faces and then silence
When a homeless person
Comes by through the carriage asking for change
(With no such concern or glance).

This time zone interference is everyday
Reality of crushing threads
Of so many nameless but named citizens
On the crossing into uncertainty.

Pressure is up tenfold; unrest is brewing
In the principle of being.
Breathing revolutions and the floods
Keep coming in actuality
Of a mass disorder through everyone going down.
No time to fight but see you
At the mind for the barricades arcade.

THE WHIP BACK (AN INDIVIDUAL'S CRY)

Well, I say what on earth is going on?
In these words, I will call out, those circling the ground.
What I saw last night just impounded any
Feelings I have for those lost.

One person singing with headphones in
And dancing on the spot,
Just so out of tune, but enjoying their moment
And maybe should have gone.
Carry bag nearby on the ground filled with beer cans,
Never causing too much fuss.

Saw the taunts start from a nearby
Gang made up of both sexes,
All outside the rubber chicken joint.

First came one just standing and staring up close,
Rather bullish in their act.
Someone came kicking the carrying bag nearby,
Spreading its contents all over.

The out of tune singing went on, just dancing on the spot.
Others came pulling at the earphones,
Grabbing at the clothing,
A whip back and then carries on
Should have just moved away,
The pack was now out on a blood in the draw.

The out of tune singer went over to them
With some kind of feather,
As the taunts continued from some women
In the pack trying to move them
Down a less public space away from the public square.
Yeah, right from a distance
I can see how this is being played out,
Ending in some form of smashing or other
Sad act in off screen brutality.

This person continues on the singing,
Dancing to their own beats.

Then some circling masked boy strides
In with a quick jerk
And circling back in some empty triumph,
The earphone man is down on the floor.
Shock now reeling down on the ground and
Then he runs off up the road.
I stare from the bus stop with a silent hex
On those that perpetrate this…
I thought fuck, what the fuck has it come to
In the mentality of the pack.
Yeah, I could see blood
In those taunts lacking distinctiveness.
Blood on those who can't clear the thoughts
So sad the pack,
No one now do or stay as no individuals be.

At the time fears to express
Except these words now I speak.
Part of a pack, part of nothing,
I'm spitting out the words.
Empty striding,
Fuck you I can't stand
This bullying,
It's just empty loss.
These directional shouts internalised
Crying out for the victimised.
I will shout out any wrong doing,
Up against it for those that are forever side-lined.
In out of tune cries, just stand-up dancing upon a spot.

SPIRITS OF PLACE ONCE SO HIGH

In those days of rush, twang and step it up
When I was always mistaken for other people.
Yes, those times in the haze of 90s East London high-rise.
Views living in close edge of
Land grabs near disused public swimming baths.

In the corner shop run by a Marriot,
Yes, a spit of his brother.
Post imaging mods in Stratford mars bars
And racks of beer cans.
Smoking roll ups, dancing scraps
And discarding chip pans with blow up outtakes.

Views cut through balancing acts on board
The light conveyor of estate horizon.
Some days just stick in your head outside
That waiting on the Wick platform
Between the nuclear waste trains and shouting gangs.

Months before I had moved up then
Out into suburbs then back into the south.
Having connected a place in Dulwich
In continued flux having not quite moved in.
Moved my entire vinyl collections up from SW,
Thinking then it was stable
Living with some newfound friends outside
The ones I had in music circles.

Through Green Park Restaurant Connections.
St Etienne's Avenue
On the personal tape speaker,
Sheep skin revival.

Mist haze morning rise taking that commute
To operate the dish machines, prep
On the Christmas office party circuit.
Lordship Lane, Elephant and Castle
And then the walk on down some alleys.

Those overnight expresses
Taking Shepherds Market in 1992,
On the steps just needing some time
To look for new lodgings.
The temp board was coming close to ending
Whilst contracts hadn't been signed.
Then the restaurant boss's Mexican break
Was about to happen.

Passing on his entire high-rise squat in Hillmorton Point,
16 floors up over the Eastway end bend.
Saying initially, it was only to look after for just one year.

A break that was needed had arrived.
Time was running low.
Organised overnight taxi to the new spot escaping
The South via smoke and mirrors.
Now with a new beginning up high.

Temporary now in hindsight.
Hanging in the staircase
If the small metal lift wasn't working.
Tip top style managing pow
A phone line on squat forecast.
Keeping it clean,
Pure connections and avoiding council evictions.

That morning in London, April 1993,
Sunny with a little breeze.
The one of many views that day that rattled
With a rising mushroom plume of smoke in the distance.
Not entirely realising what had happened until later.
As this was in the days of pre mobile smart ass news feeding.

That evening on my way to the train,
Going across using the North Link
Seeing friends in Camden.
Man running, shouting
He had lost his home that same day.
The same place it seems
As we saw the rising smoke come from.

His entire life had changed
Shouting they have blown up his home.
As it turned out he was rough camping it out
In Bishopsgate, just near Liverpool Street.
As a truck filled with explosives had blown up.
He was sleeping, hidden in a dip nearby.

Now in a flux and dazed
With shock of the unimaginable.
To this day still I am unsure
How he got to that point in meeting.

In years of hindsight, I come to thinking now maybe
Adrenalin had that power of taking hold.
Making him walk all that way out across
Parks, tracks and yards,
East to that very point.
Blurred vision in a mind's eye.
Grasping the time gone,
Walking through another account deep inside the blast.
A chain of events in a vacuum of time.

Spirit movement in flux
On to the hospital down on Homerton Grove.
Seemed to be the best thing to do.
Since shock was highlighted as a bigger killer.

A visitation to go back the next day,
But no one was there.
This troubled spirit had moved in passing on park dew.
Morning train back to the SW home several years later
To view a demolition filmed in artist
Interpretation through those eastern estates.

Ghosts on Retreat Place come
Forth in enhanced templates.
Years on abstracted footage coming up later in
'Friends from the north'.

Those triggers on reading
An artistic observation and recognition of characters.
Concrete filled interior moulds to decipher human patterns.

Taking it back on the record
Its cycle to repeat over and over
In a mind that's split, talking in verges and out of context.
Spirits of a place once so high
Now holding so very still.

BLINK MY EYE AND SEE YOUR SHADOW PLAY

Golden leaves up in deep cold
Murmurs over the hearth on slow
Residue of where you sat
Noises of your sound
Ring round the room

Down the river warren
Burrow deep and slow
My furrows through the lost
And then another
Sounds of you lay deep
In tape and piano resonance

I hear you call in a distant voice
Over misted tracks simultaneously
Just after a horn is blown through the morning
In the folds of time
Semi lucid laying here
To witness the shift and clouds
Crack coming in worlds between
Your voice calls my name

In this time the bells ring out
And circle the round
Through letters of a name
In time I look up and it pours with light.

Golden sparks sitting on the rim of the day
Haven is where it is
Searching under foot
The sorrow floats on howls
Your voice rang clear
We sing in thank you with greeting hay

Each and every other passing
We still think of the one love
True to the residues left

Deep roots down and pictures framed in mind
Boxes of items collected paperwork scars
And more photos deep in mystic

Ice disc in the bend of the river
A day of passing
I blink my eye and see the shadows play
In the residues of the extant.

TAKE IT BACK FROM **THE SHOUT HOUSE**

Years of misguided feelings coming out into the light.
What is actually happening here and why?
These questions need to be sought and brought.

Truth Cabs roaming the streets, historical bites floating,
For those that need to know their sources.
We don't need a time machine to see the Nazis!

It's already here test marketing hate across the lands,
Used children in cages
Taken at the borders in enforced separations.
Seeing how the public react and dare I say it,
On how they will take these extremes
Onward to un-imaginable horrors.

Simultaneous shouts for a freedom of speech,
Out bursts just twisted and ever so misleading
It's you they are wanting.
The brink on the right house stirring pots,
Conjuring boils and diverting your mind revisions.

Those exit casting shadows over the land,
Now building open chasms of division.
Beatings in the street upon the opening gaps,
Fuelled on by a Sun in the Mail Expressions
And now the deep dark socials X and more.

Using the working people
All people as tools
To gain further blind sight.
Fabric seeping cracks in the hardball terrace.
Marches into riot rot hotel skirmish
In the shells rising below the surface.
Incidents happening over and over,
Ever so close into the border.

Proclaiming a freedom of speech
That if those powers were reached,
Nothing but restriction would be in place.
Unsavoury in the long lines, taking of bookmarks,
We have to remember our pages.

The Shout House stirred up to roar,
Drip feeding hate into the system.
Insular throughout,
A building of some false patriot stock.
Shut ups increasing rattling on its last,
Lies being up-scaled,
But paid up and backed to continue into the horizon.

Laid bare in the drivel
That's driving those forces.
Finding the money
That pays this hatred,
Our Carnival of Resistance keeps breaking it down.

The shot of many times crossing
It's on a constant edit…
Party's that you once trusted seem twisted.
In the Laws they make what you say do illegal
Taking it back from the Shout House.
Signalling through on bright sparks,
Paving a way to enhance a truth of co-existence with all.

A true collective DIY resistance
Outside the technocratic boiling points.
A need to use the cracks upon that ingrained surface.
Speak out and break the hate, deep down,
Share and stand at the crossing of frantic flag beating.

SUNDAY CROSSING IN A DOWNPOUR

Twisting the public's mind in a cause and dispute,
Whilst bookending the undercover spy tales.
Putting blame up onto the most obvious trail,
Oblivious to any missing letters.

Big time business in omni rewrites,
Spreading the corporate shift in treacherous highlights.
The harvest is here upon us
With engineers playing out the theatrical web.

Blinding public broadcast in fragile wrappings,
Howls of a cover up, view seasons in outbursts.
Speeches about turn and twists it to put blame on you.

Nest of vipers, abstract conditions
Evoke the bottomless depths sinking,
Maintaining that power, corruption and treason.

We need to operate the cog machine
Somewhere near listing.
Sunday crossings in a downpour,
Bridging a psyche outside those responsible.

Proper fantastic fanfare,
Blossoms on the common
Behind the low enforcement.

Were there sightings
Amongst the dog walkers,
Phone users and those passing?
Beholding in the truth amongst them
Flat out within double-dealings.
Up on circus west village with vistas over the tracks,
Observing of the high appointments.

Glasshouses funding from oblivion up high and sunny.
Waste excreting through weapons exporting.
Now with those all above
In some lay of a land and law.
Somehow the dystopian novel has now come alive
Outside the library halls, taskmasters battering
Those from fiction to facts.
Negatively charged Ions
Attracting the particles of poisoned dust.

The stars are circling rights of the species,
Keeping an eye like hawks in the skies.
Morning there's two suits with one imputing notes
And the other shifting behind.
Security man now passing
Singing *keeping the dream alive…*

I SAW THE WHISTLERS OF THE LAND

I heard the whistlers of the land
When they came and took our hearts and souls
Songs sung in the breadth deep in mind.

In the deep dark land's storms rage
The monsters come and go
But I hold a vision inside through song…

Fields high and low through rivers gathered
In time the light, will I feel your face inside
It continues and holding on to the
Whistlers of the land.
Those whistlers of the land…
Seeing in time and a change through all…

The whistlers of the land
Tempo reacts
The whistlers of the land
Cracks through the sound
The whistlers of the land
Community stand
The whistlers of the land…

www.ingramcontent.com/pod-product-compliance
Lightning Source LLC
LaVergne TN
LVHW020048110826
845155LV00029B/691

* 9 7 8 1 9 1 1 2 3 2 6 4 3 *